BILLY JOEL

Cover photo © Getty Images / Paul Natkin / Contributor

ISBN 978-1-5400-8436-1

Visit Hal Leonard Online at
www.halleonard.com

Contact us:
Hal Leonard
7777 West Bluemound Road
Milwaukee, WI 53213
Email: info@halleonard.com

In Europe, contact:
Hal Leonard Europe Limited
42 Wigmore Street
Marylebone, London, W1U 2RN
Email: info@halleonardeurope.com

In Australia, contact:
Hal Leonard Australia Pty. Ltd.
4 Lentara Court
Cheltenham, Victoria, 3192 Australia
Email: info@halleonard.com.au

Welcome to the *Super Easy Songbook* series!

This unique collection will help you play your favorite songs quickly and easily. Here's how it works:

- Play the simplified melody with your right hand. Letter names appear inside each note to assist you.

- There are no key signatures to worry about! If a sharp ♯ or flat ♭ is needed, it is shown beside the note each time.

- There are no page turns, so your hands never have to leave the keyboard.

- If two notes are connected by a tie ⌣, hold the first note for the combined number of beats. (The second note does not show a letter name since it is not re-struck.)

- Add basic chords with your left hand using the provided keyboard diagrams. Chord voicings have been carefully chosen to minimize hand movement.

- The left-hand rhythm is up to you, and chord notes can be played together or separately. Be creative!

- If the chords sound muddy, move your left hand an octave* higher. If this gets in the way of playing the melody, move your right hand an octave higher as well.

    An octave spans eight notes. If your starting note is C, the next C to the right is an octave higher.

———————————— ALSO AVAILABLE ————————————

Hal Leonard Student Keyboard Guide HL00296039

Key Stickers HL00100016

Allentown

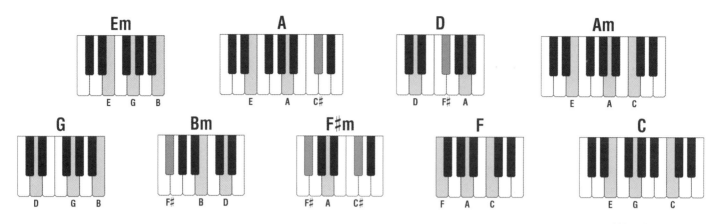

Words and Music by
Billy Joel

Moderately

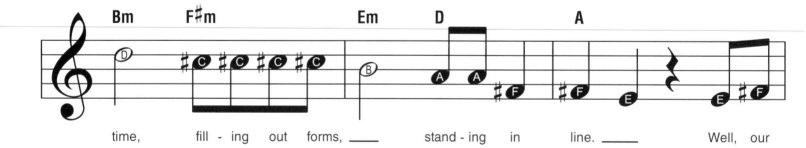

Well, we're liv - ing here in Al - len - town, and they're

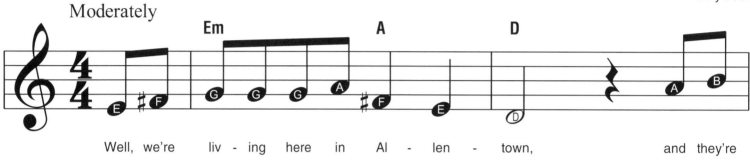

clos - ing all the fac - to - ries down. Out in Beth - le - hem, they're kill - ing

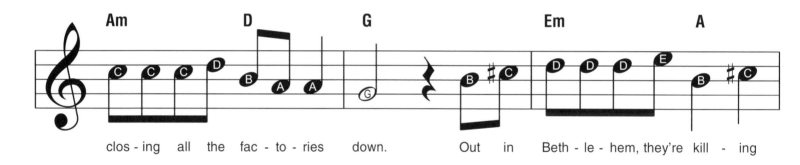

time, fill - ing out forms, stand - ing in line. Well, our

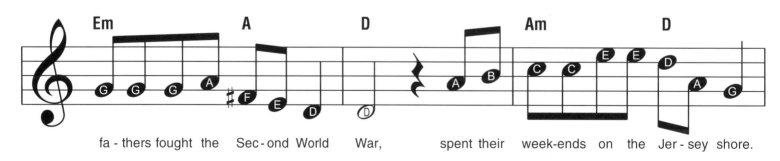

fa - thers fought the Sec - ond World War, spent their week - ends on the Jer - sey shore.

Met our moth - ers in the U - S - O, asked them to

dance, dance with them slow. ____ And we're liv - ing here in Al - len - town, _

____ but the rest - less - ness was hand - ed ____ down. And it's

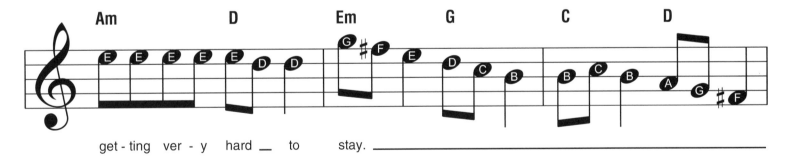

get - ting ver - y hard __ to stay. _____

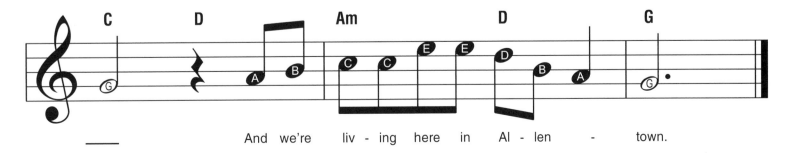

____ And we're liv - ing here in Al - len - town.

And So It Goes

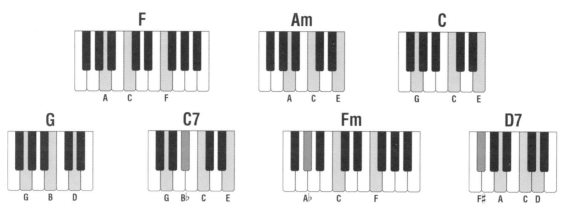

Words and Music by
Billy Joel

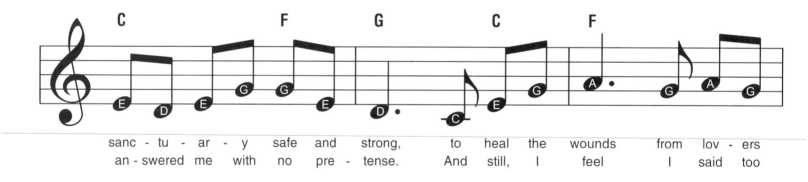

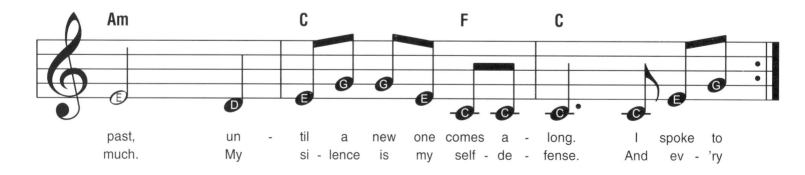

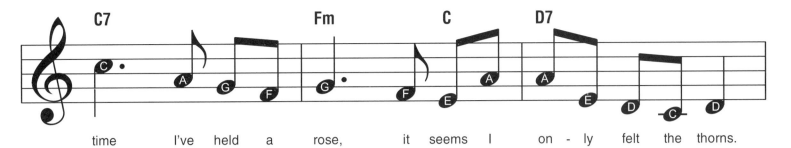

time I've held a rose, it seems I on - ly felt the thorns.

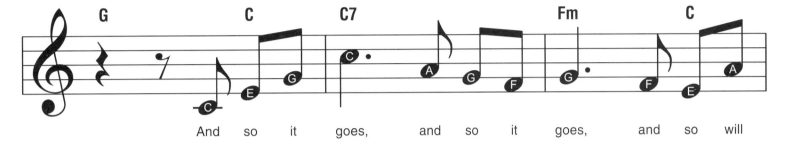

And so it goes, and so it goes, and so will

you soon, I sup - pose. But if my si - lence made you

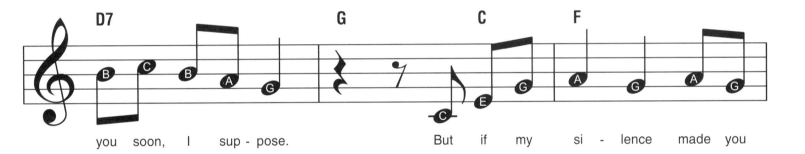

leave, then that would be my worst mis - take. So, I will

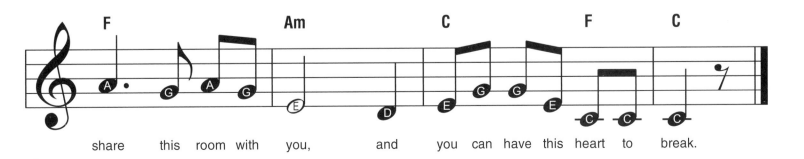

share this room with you, and you can have this heart to break.

Don't Ask Me Why

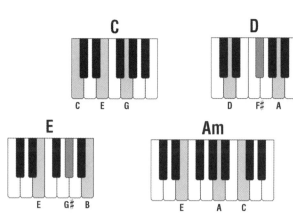
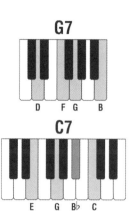
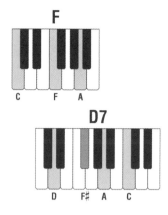

Words and Music by
Billy Joel

Moderate half-time feel

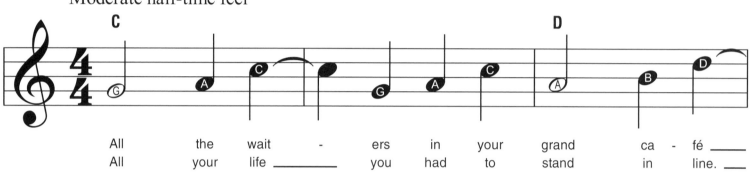

All the wait - ers in your grand ca - fé _____
All your life _____ you had to grand stand in line. ___

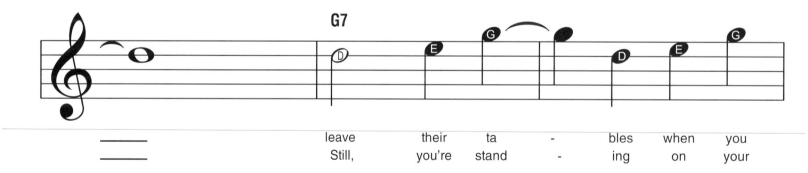

_____ leave their ta - bles when you
_____ Still, you're stand - ing on your

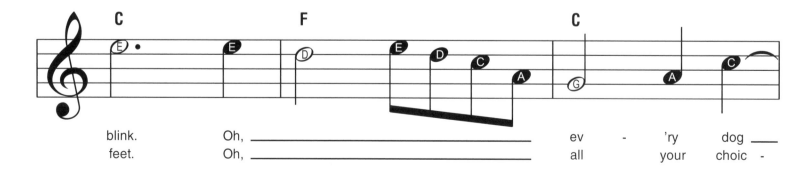

blink. Oh, _____ ev - 'ry dog _____
feet. Oh, _____ all your choic -

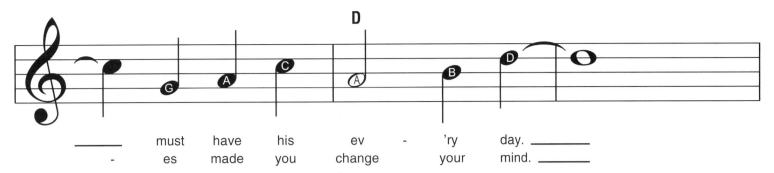

_____ must have his ev - 'ry day. _____
- es made you change your mind. _____

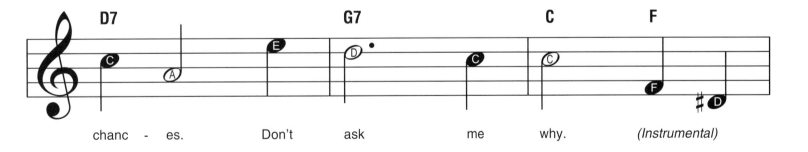

Ev - 'ry drunk _____ must have his drink.
Now your cal - en - dar's com - plete. Don't

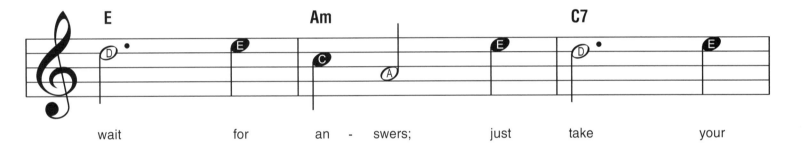

wait for an - swers; just take your

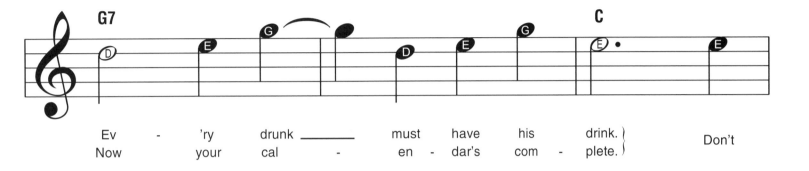

chanc - es. Don't ask me why. *(Instrumental)*

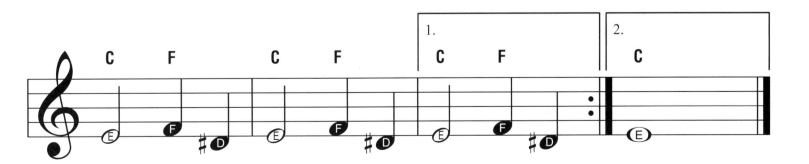

Honesty

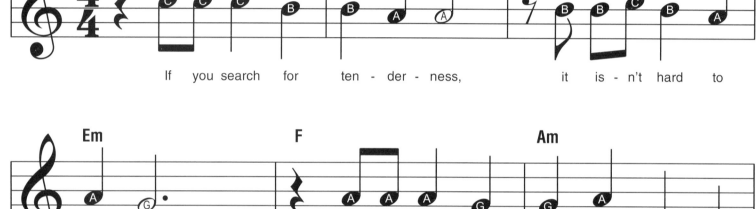

Words and Music by
Billy Joel

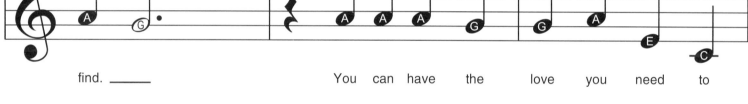

Moderately slow

If you search for ten - der - ness, it is - n't hard to

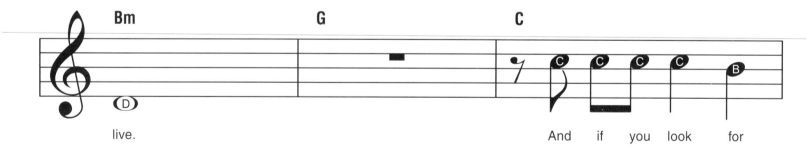

find. _____ You can have the love you need to

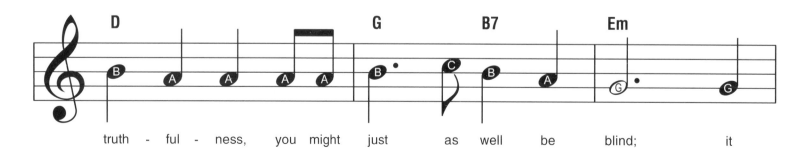

live. And if you look for

truth - ful - ness, you might just as well be blind; it

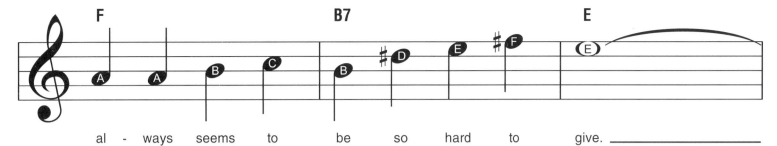

al - ways seems to be so hard to give. _____

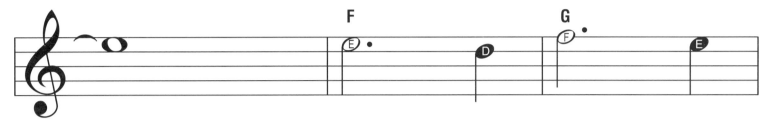

_____ Hon - es - ty is

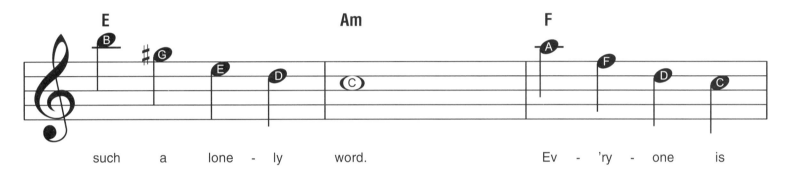

such a lone - ly word. Ev - 'ry - one is

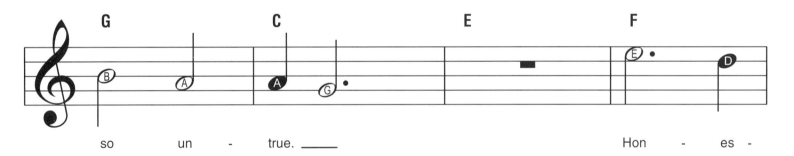

so un - true. _____ Hon - es -

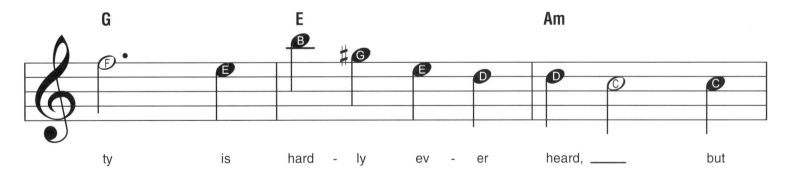

ty is hard - ly ev - er heard, _____ but

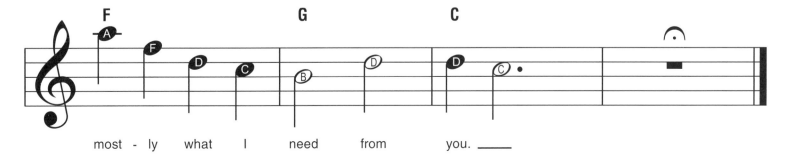

most - ly what I need from you. _____

It's Still Rock and Roll to Me

Additional Lyrics

3. How about a pair of pink side-winders
   And a bright orange pair of pants?
   "Well, you could really be a Beau Brummel, baby,
   If you just give it half a chance.

Don't waste your money on a new set of speakers,
You get more mileage from a cheap pair of sneakers."
Next phase, new wave, dance craze, anyways,
It's still rock and roll to me.

Just the Way You Are

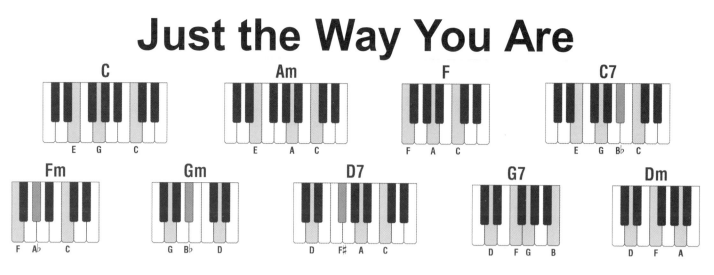

Words and Music by
Billy Joel

Moderately fast

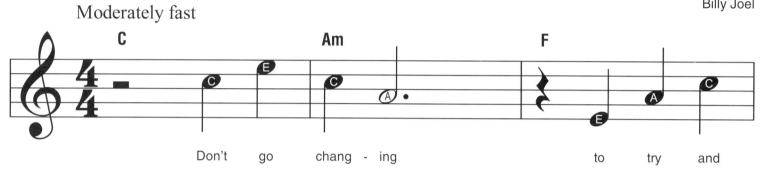

Don't go chang-ing to try and

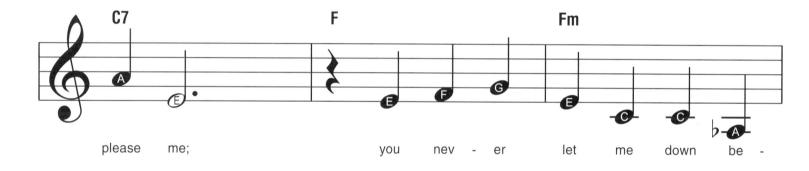

please me; you nev - er let me down be -

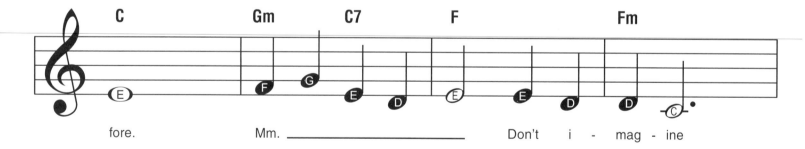

fore. Mm. _____ Don't i - mag - ine

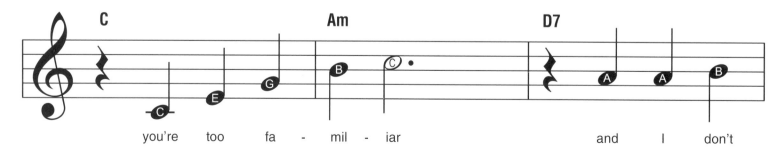

you're too fa - mil - iar and I don't

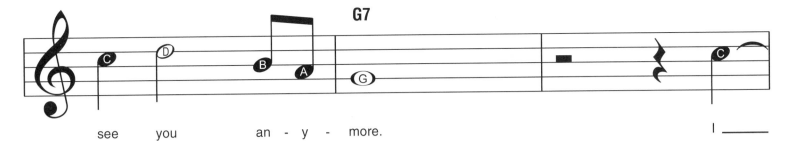

see you an - y - more. I ____

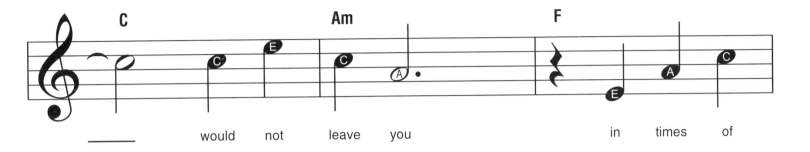

____ would not leave you in times of

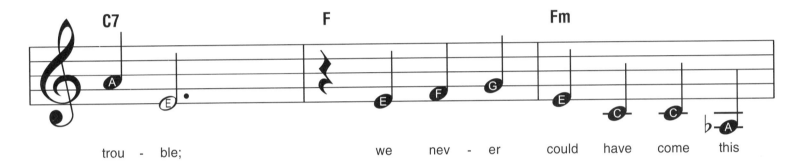

trou - ble; we nev - er could have come this

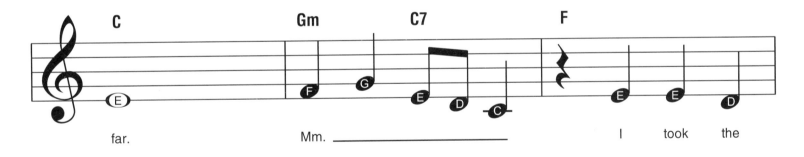

far. Mm. ____ I took the

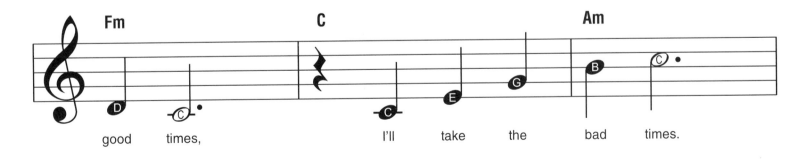

good times, I'll take the bad times.

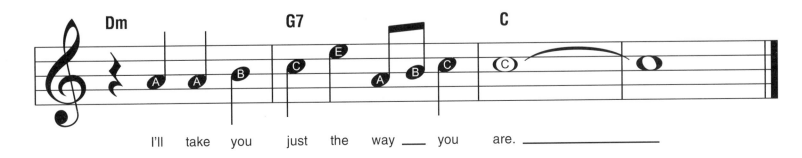

I'll take you just the way ____ you are. ____

Keeping the Faith

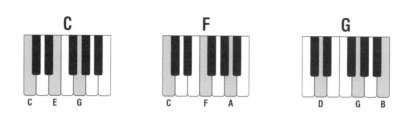

Words and Music by
Billy Joel

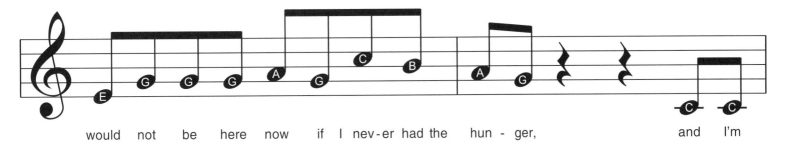

would not be here now if I nev-er had the hun-ger, and I'm

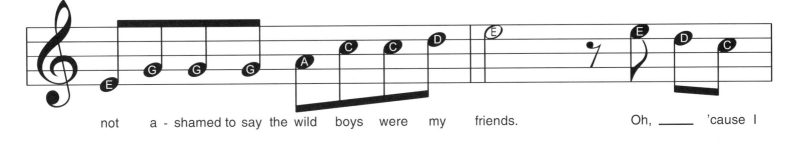

not a - shamed to say the wild boys were my friends. Oh, ____ 'cause I

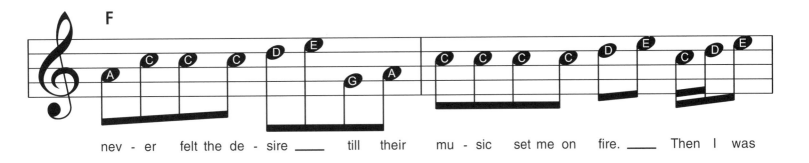

nev - er felt the de - sire ____ till their mu - sic set me on fire. ____ Then I was

saved, yeah. ____ That's why I'm keep-ing the

faith, yeah, yeah, yeah, yeah, keep-ing the faith. ____

The Longest Time

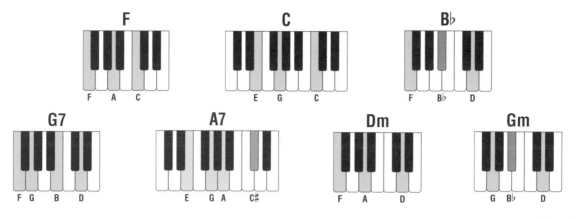

Words and Music by
Billy Joel

Moderate half-time feel

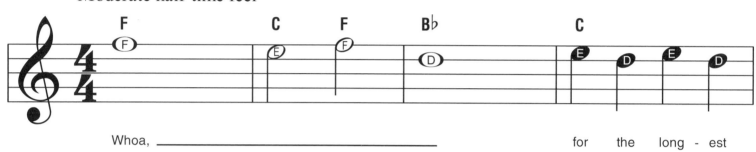

Whoa, _____ for the long - est

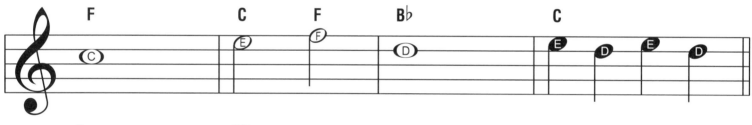

time. Whoa, _____ for the long - est...

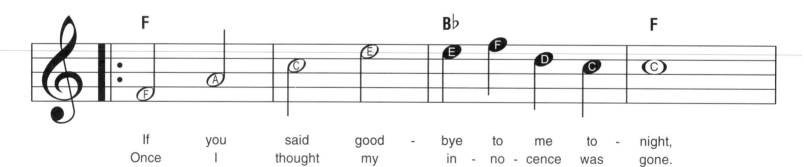

If you said good - bye to me to - night,
Once I thought my in - no - cence was gone.

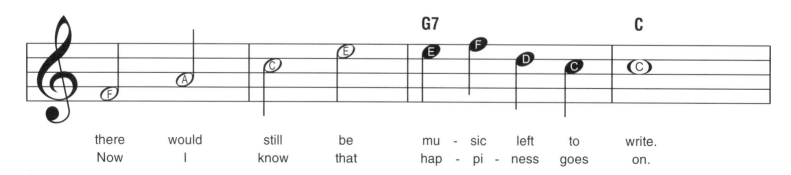

there would still be mu - sic left to write.
Now I know that hap - pi - ness goes on.

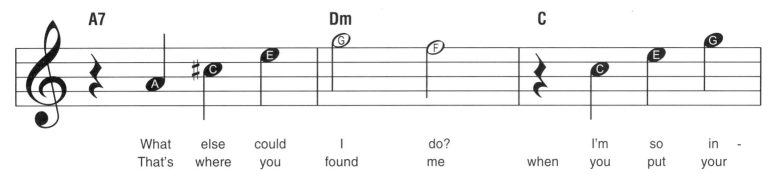

What else could I do? I'm so in -
That's where you I found me when you put your

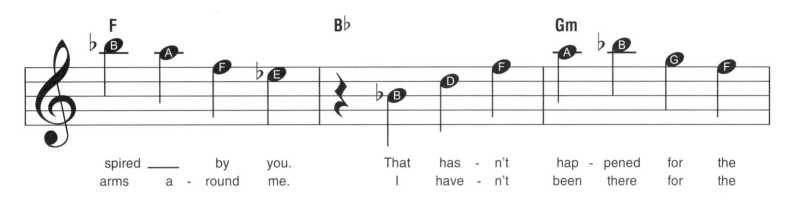

spired _____ by you.
arms a - round me.

That has - n't hap - pened for the
I have - n't been there for the

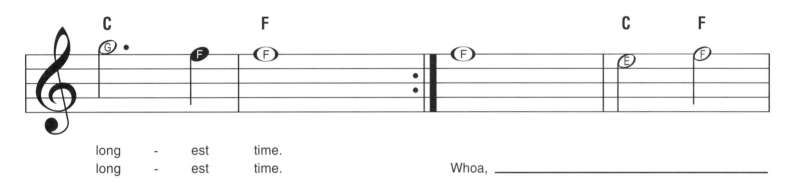

long - est time.
long - est time.

Whoa, _____

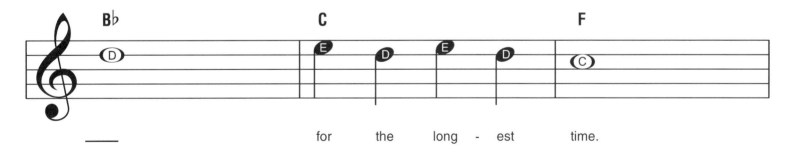

_____ for the long - est time.

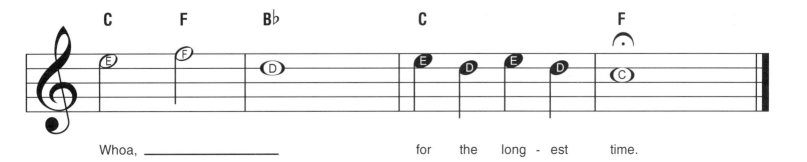

Whoa, _____ for the long - est time.

Lullabye
(Goodnight, My Angel)

Words and Music by
Billy Joel

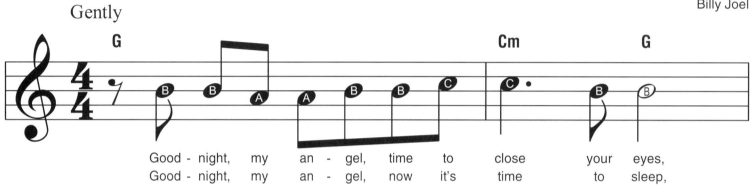

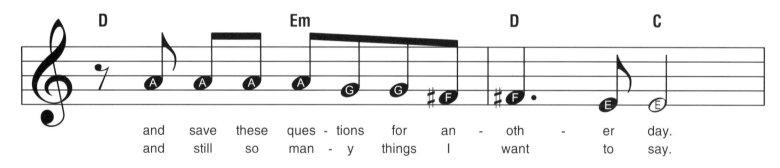

Movin' Out
(Anthony's Song)

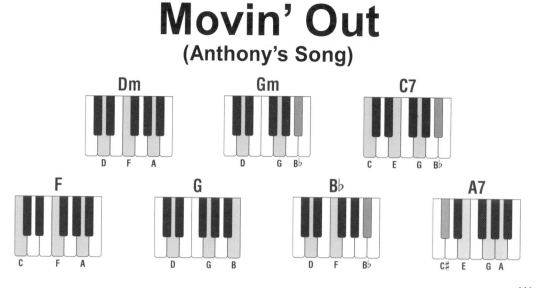

Words and Music by
Billy Joel

Moderately fast

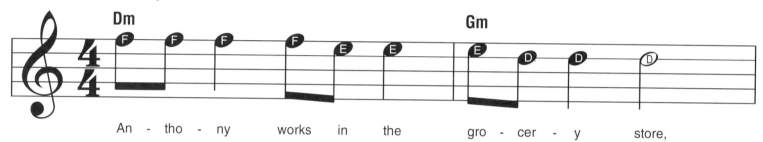

An - tho - ny works in the gro - cer - y store,

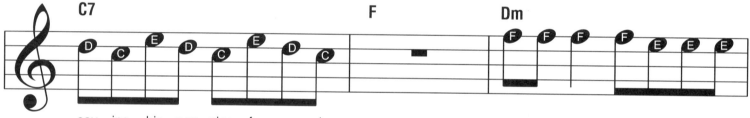

sav - ing his pen - nies for some - day. Ma - ma Le - o - ni left a

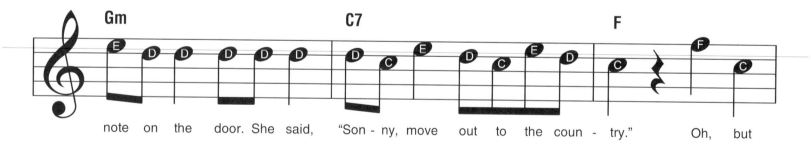

note on the door. She said, "Son - ny, move out to the coun - try." Oh, but

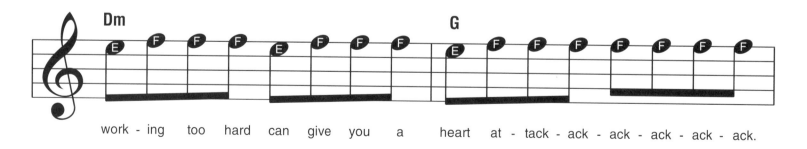

work - ing too hard can give you a heart at - tack - ack - ack - ack - ack - ack.

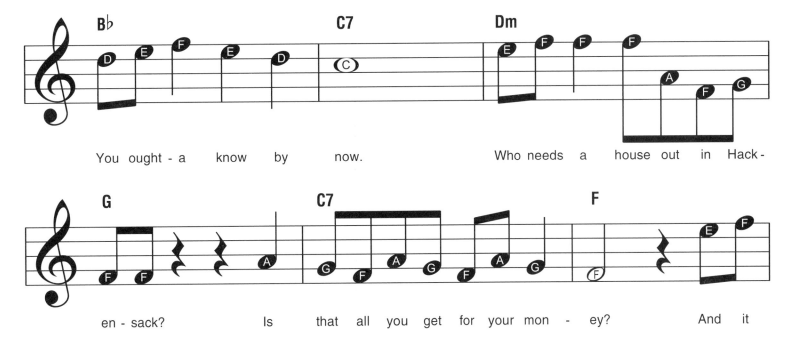

You ought - a know by now. Who needs a house out in Hack -

en - sack? Is that all you get for your mon - ey? And it

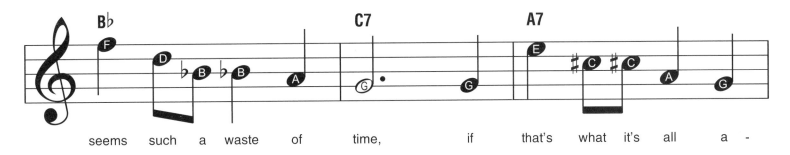

seems such a waste of time, if that's what it's all a -

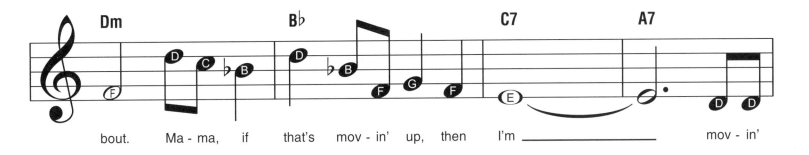

bout. Ma - ma, if that's mov - in' up, then I'm _____ mov - in'

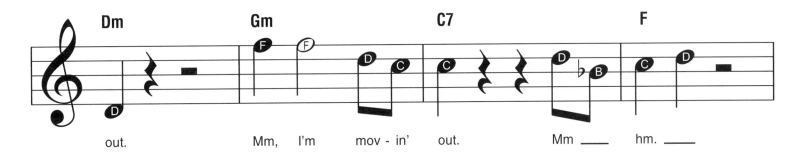

out. Mm, I'm mov - in' out. Mm ___ hm. ___

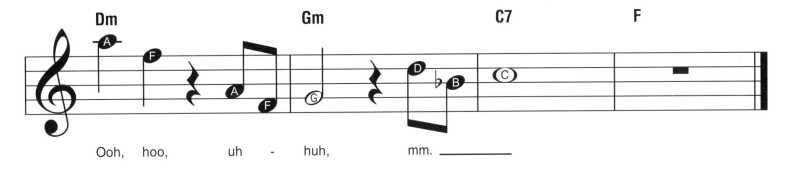

Ooh, hoo, uh - huh, mm. _____

My Life

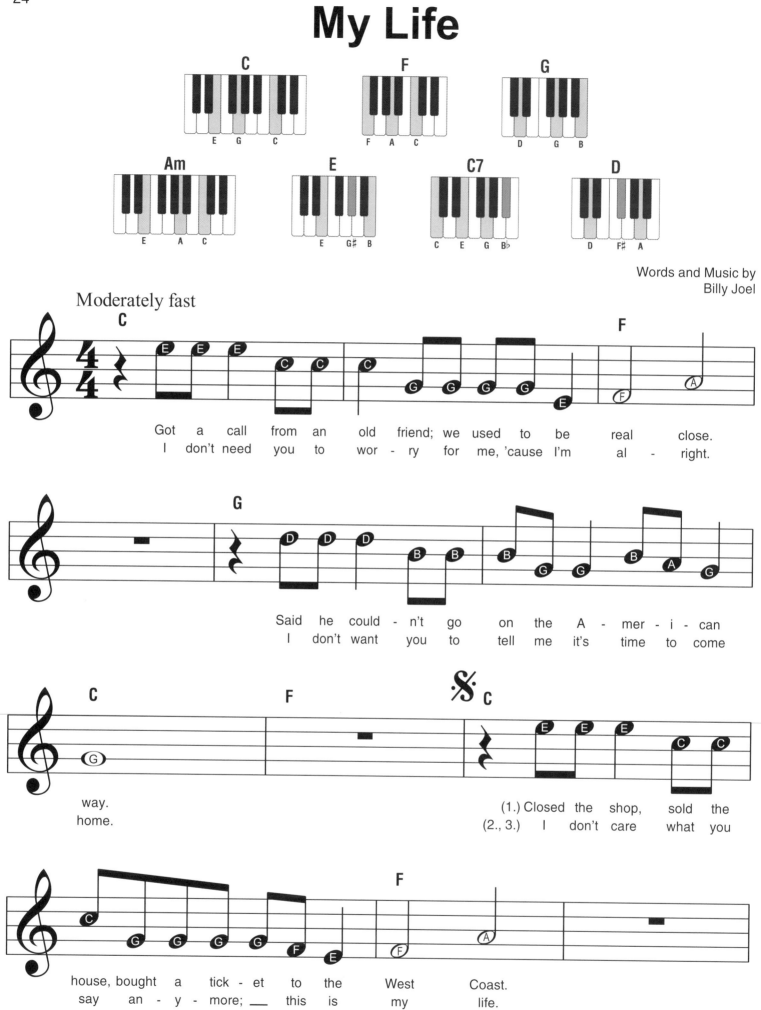

Words and Music by
Billy Joel

New York State of Mind

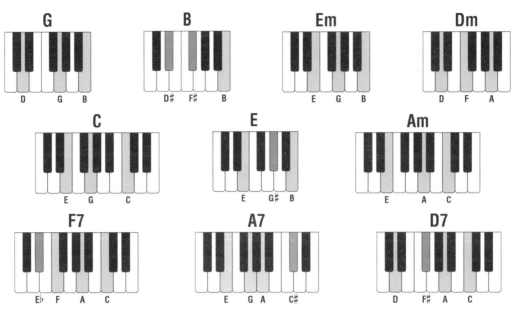

Words and Music by
Billy Joel

Slow Blues feel

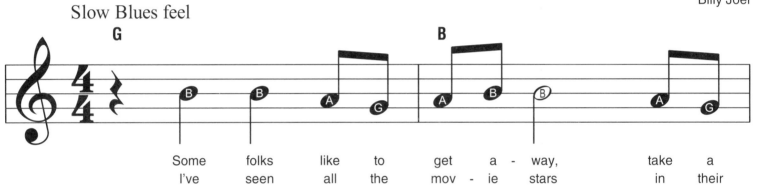

Some folks like to get a - way, take a
I've seen all the mov - ie stars in their

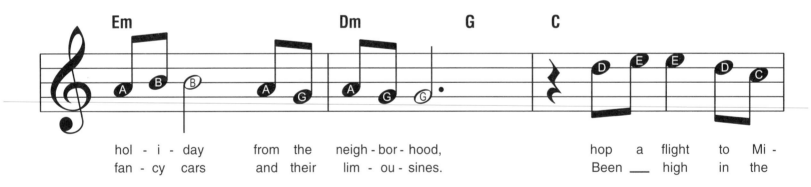

hol - i - day from the neigh - bor - hood, hop a flight to Mi -
fan - cy cars and their lim - ou - sines. Been ___ high in the

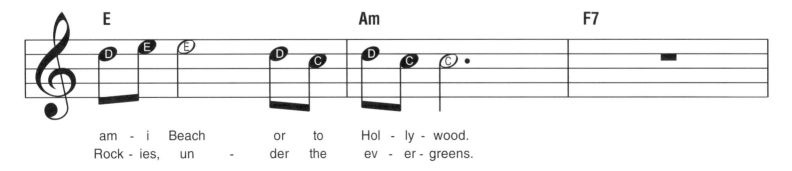

am - i Beach or to Hol - ly - wood.
Rock - ies, un - der the ev - er - greens.

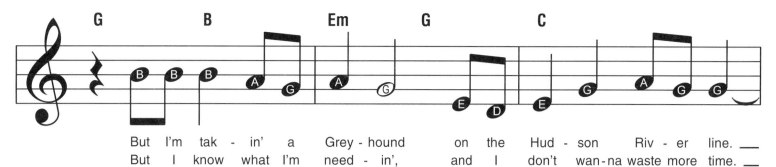

But I'm tak - in' a Grey - hound on the Hud - son Riv - er line. ___
But I know what I'm need - in', and I don't wan-na waste more time. ___

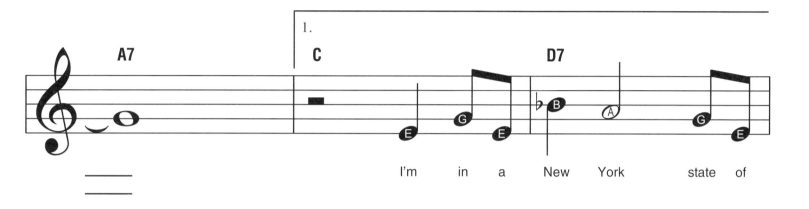

_____ I'm in a New York state of

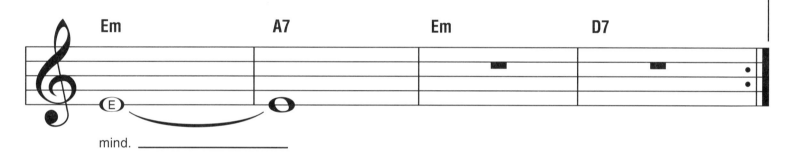

mind. _____

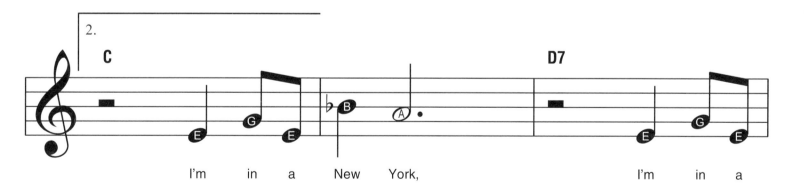

I'm in a New York, I'm in a

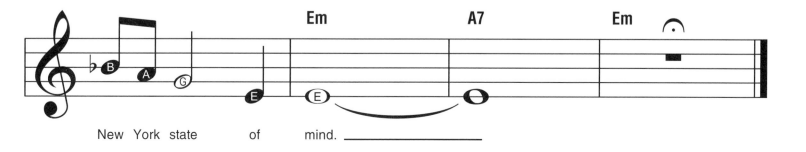

New York state of mind. _____

Only the Good Die Young

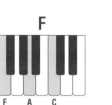 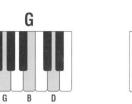 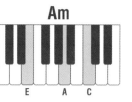 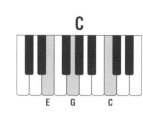 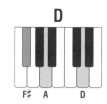

Words and Music by
Billy Joel

Piano Man

Words and Music by
Billy Joel

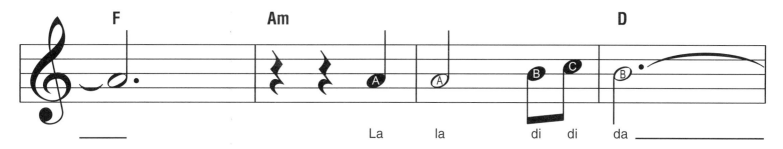

La la di di da _____

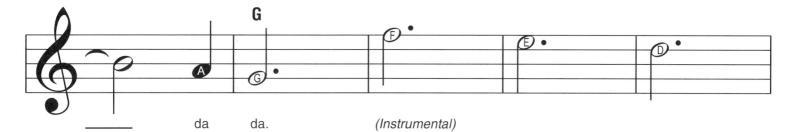

da da. _____ *(Instrumental)*

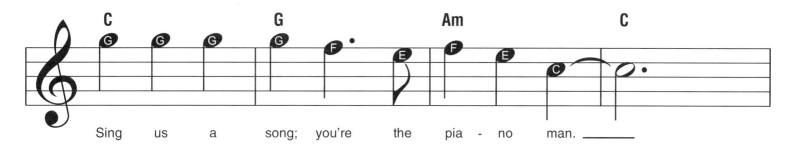

Sing us a song; you're the pia - no man. _____

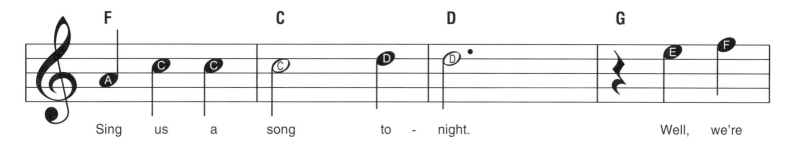

Sing us a song to - night. Well, we're

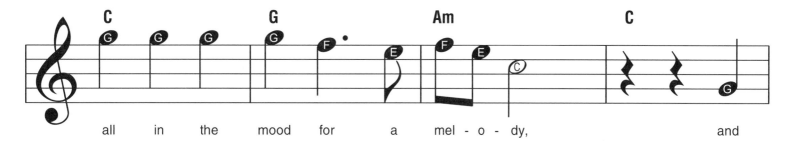

all in the mood for a mel - o - dy, and

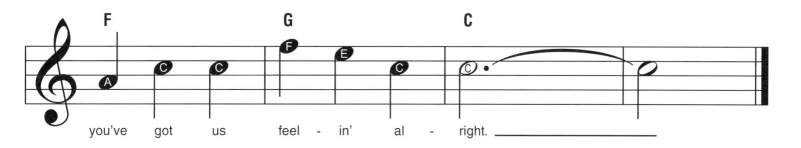

you've got us feel - in' al - right. _____

The River of Dreams

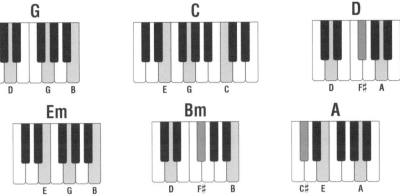

Words and Music by
Billy Joel

Smooth Shuffle

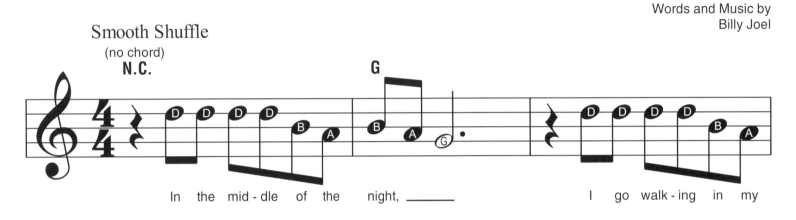

In the mid-dle of the night, _____ I go walk-ing in my

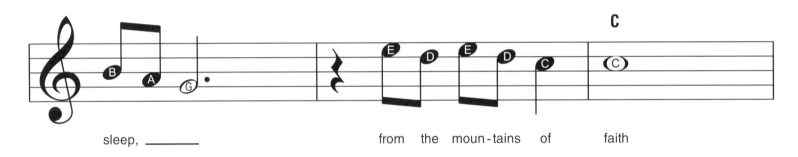

sleep, _____ from the moun-tains of faith

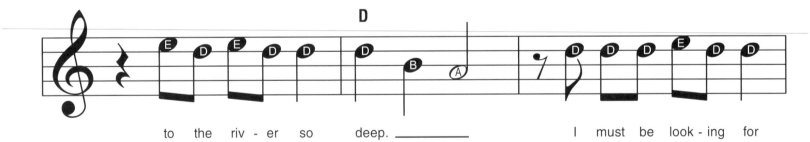

to the riv-er so deep. _____ I must be look-ing for

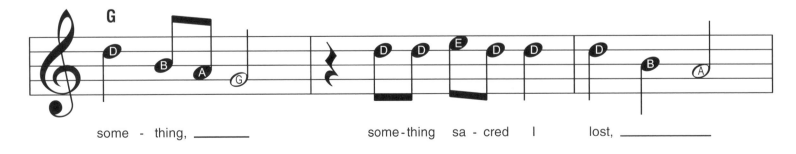

some-thing, _____ some-thing sa-cred I lost, _____

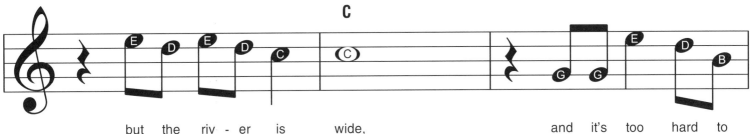

but the riv - er is wide, and it's too hard to

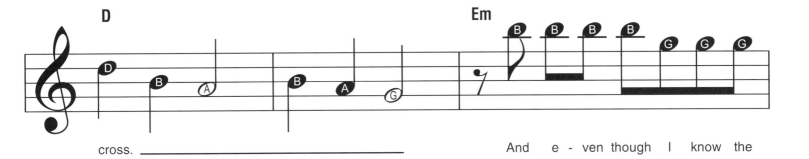

cross. _____ And e - ven though I know the

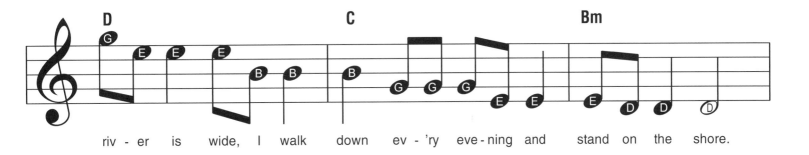

riv - er is wide, I walk down ev - 'ry eve - ning and stand on the shore.

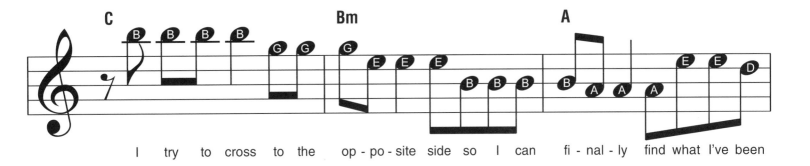

I try to cross to the op - po - site side so I can fi - nal - ly find what I've been

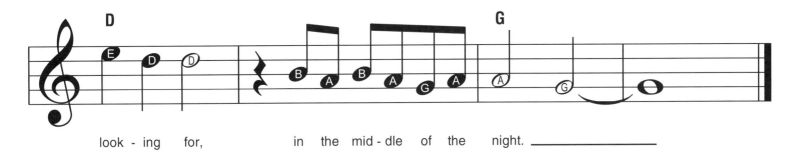

look - ing for, in the mid - dle of the night. _____

She's Always a Woman

Words and Music by
Billy Joel

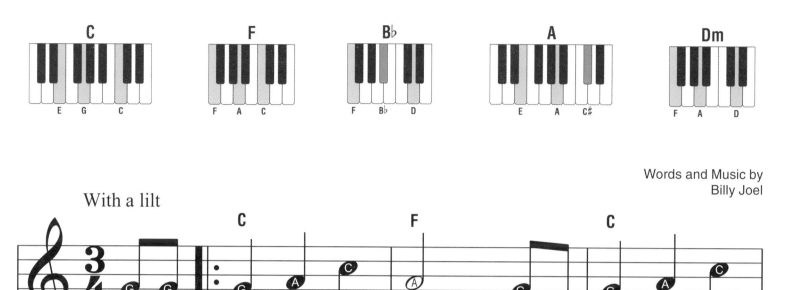

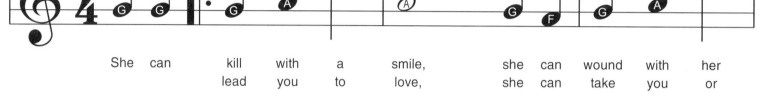

She can kill with a smile, she can wound with her
lead you to love, she can wound take you her or

eyes. _____
leave _____ you.

She can ru - in your
She can ask for the

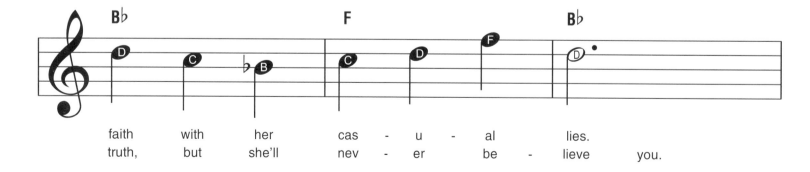

faith with her cas - u - al lies.
truth, but her she'll nev - er be - lieve you.

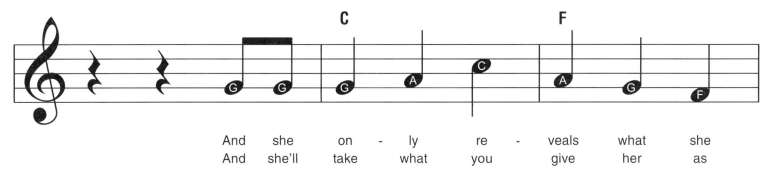

And she on - ly re - veals what she
And she'll on take - ly what you re - give her as

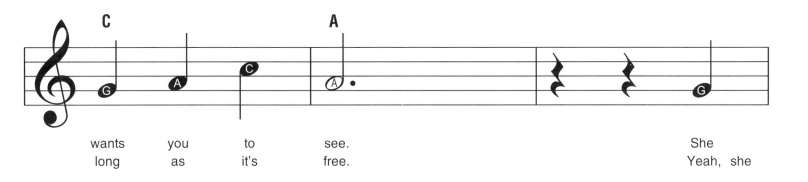

wants you to see. She
long as it's free. Yeah, she

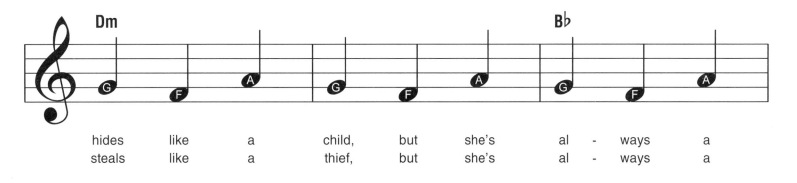

hides like a child, but she's al - ways a
steals like a thief, but she's al - ways a

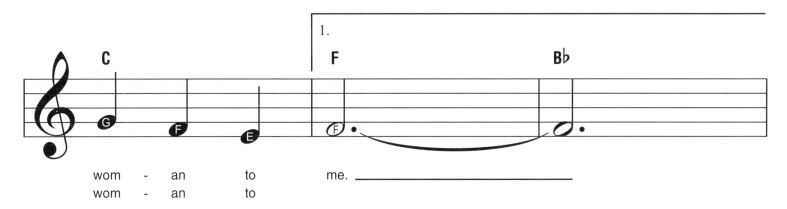

1.

wom - an to me. _____
wom - an to

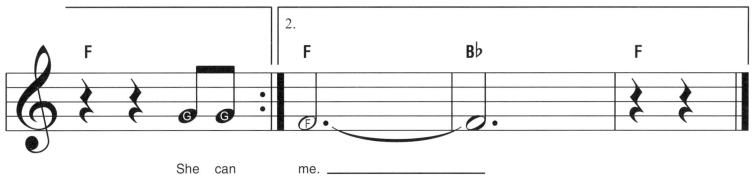

2.

She can me. _____

She's Got a Way

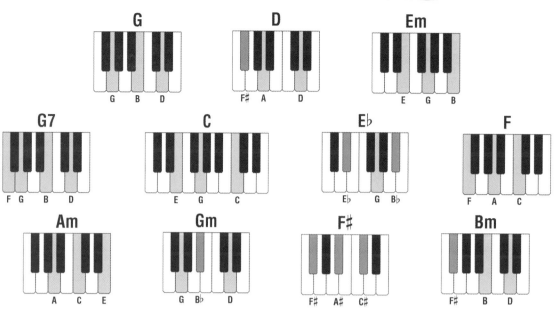

Words and Music by
Billy Joel

Slowly

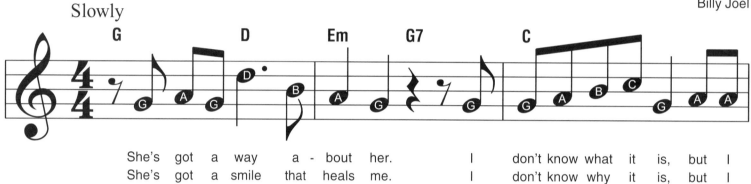

She's got a way a - bout her. I don't know what it is, but I
She's got a smile that heals me. I don't know why it is, but I

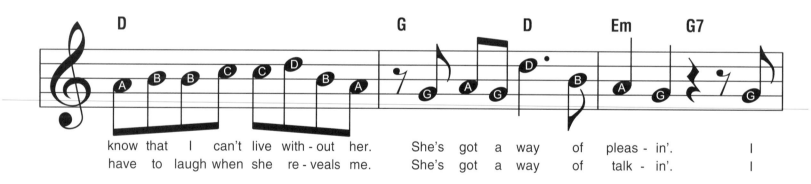

know that I can't live with - out her. She's got a way of pleas - in'. I
have to laugh when she re - veals me. She's got a way of talk - in'. I

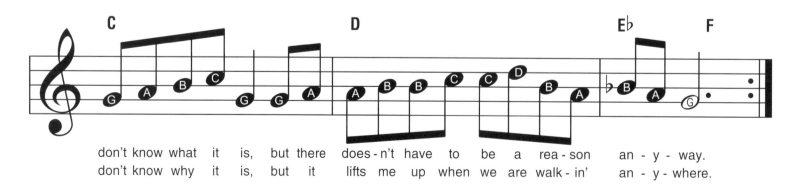

don't know what it is, but there does - n't have to be a rea - son an - y - way.
don't know why it is, but it lifts me up when we are walk - in' an - y - where.

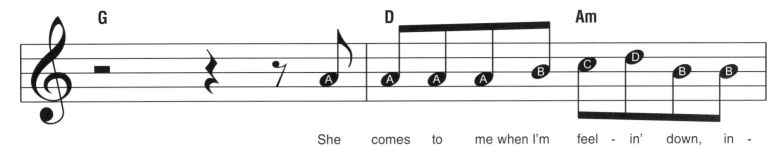

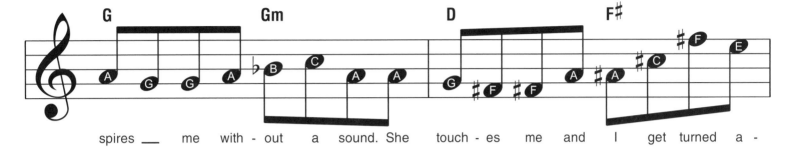

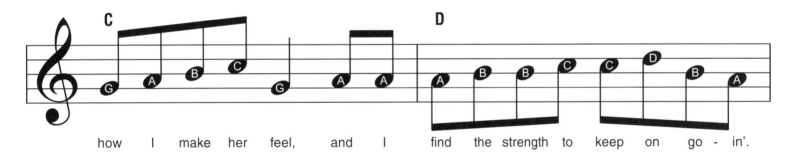

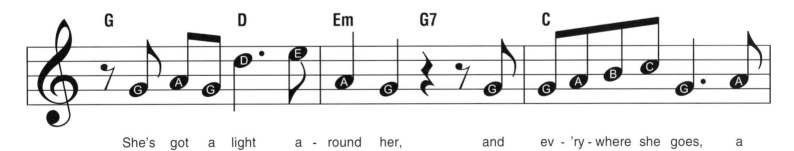

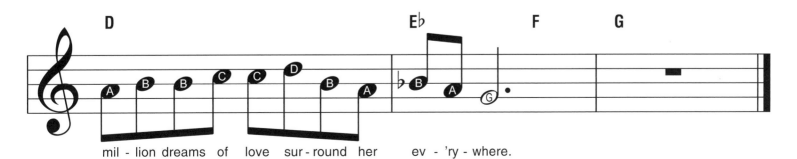

Tell Her About It

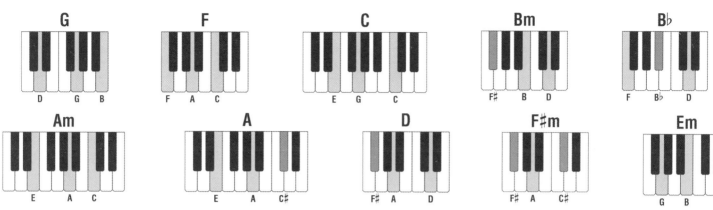

Words and Music by
Billy Joel

Bright Rock

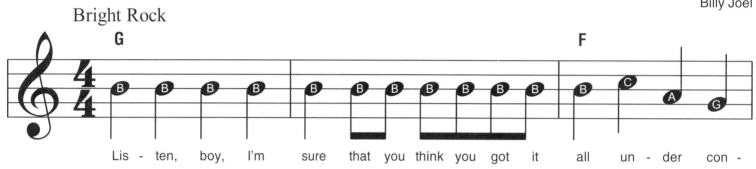

Lis - ten, boy, I'm sure that you think you got it all un - der con -

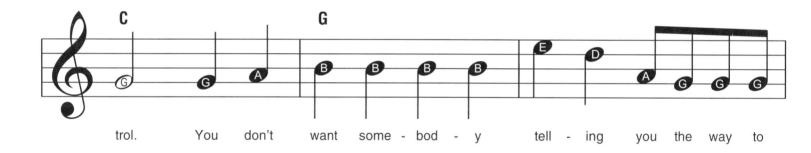

trol. You don't want some - bod - y tell - ing you the way to

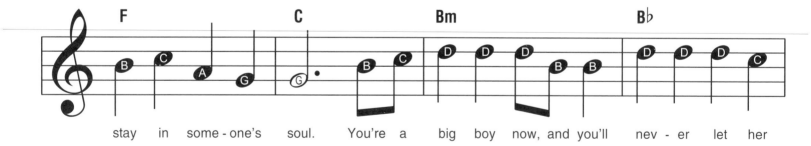

stay in some - one's soul. You're a big boy now, and you'll nev - er let her

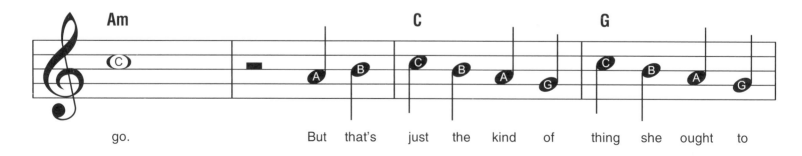

go. But that's just the kind of thing she ought to

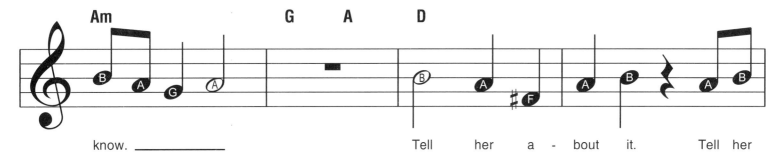

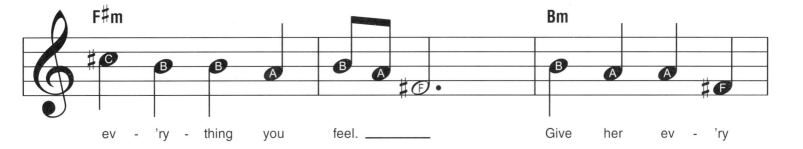

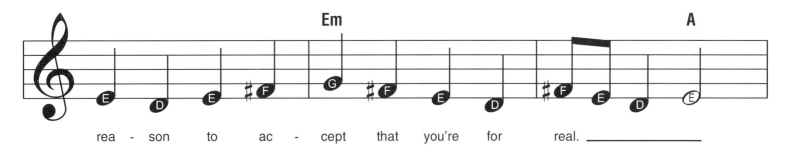

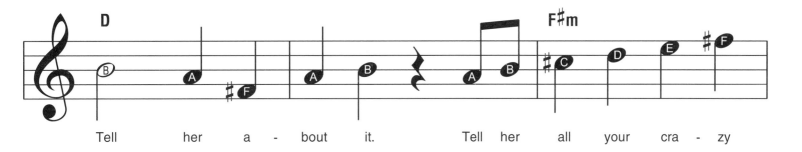

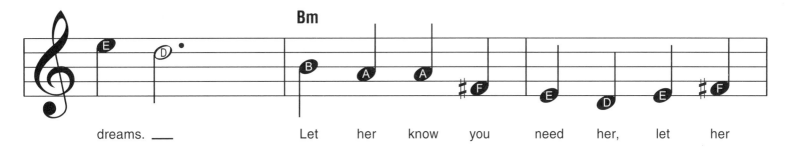

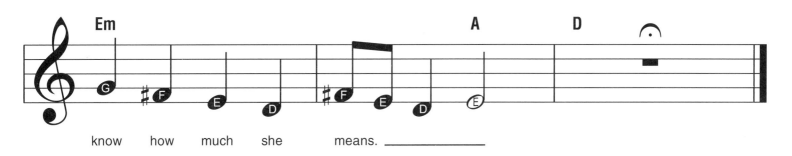

Uptown Girl

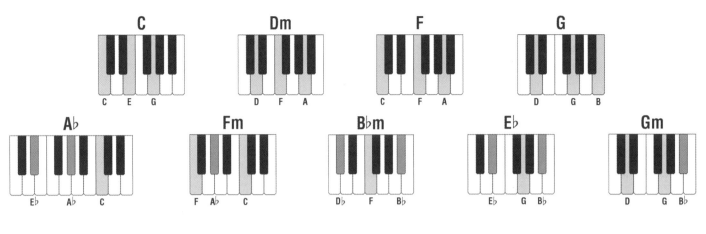

Words and Music by
Billy Joel

Moderately fast Rock

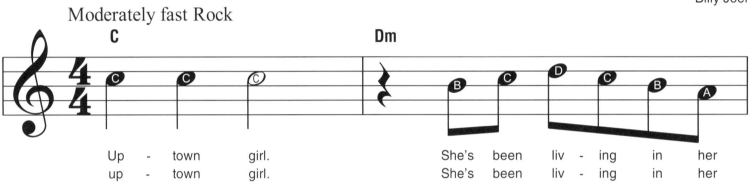

Up - town girl.　She's been liv - ing in her
up - town girl.　She's been liv - ing in her

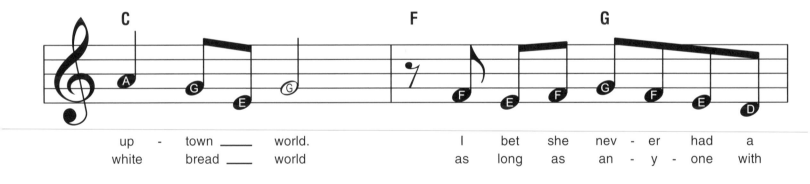

up - town _____ world.　I bet she nev - er had a
white bread _____ world　as long as an - y - one with

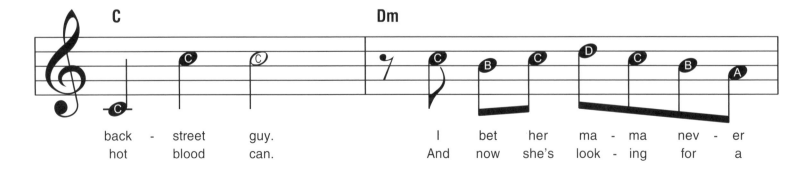

back - street guy.　I bet her ma - ma nev - er
hot blood can.　And now she's look - ing for a

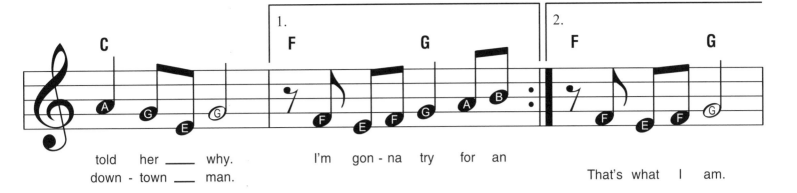

told her ___ why.   I'm gon-na try for an

down-town ___ man.   That's what I am.

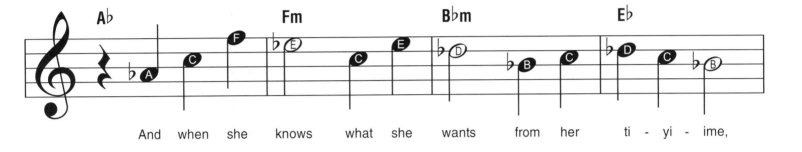

And when she knows what she wants from her ti - yi - ime,

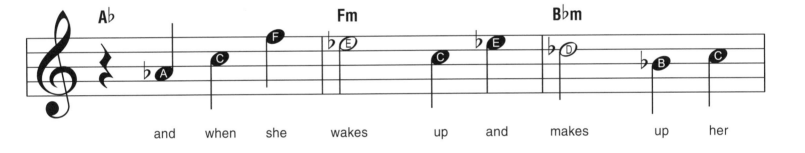

and when she wakes up and makes up her

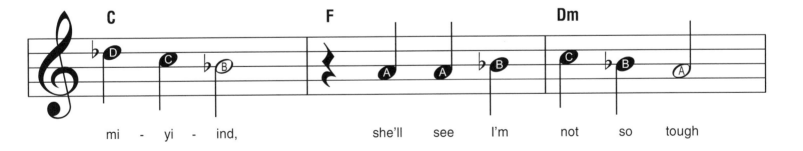

mi - yi - ind,   she'll see I'm not so tough

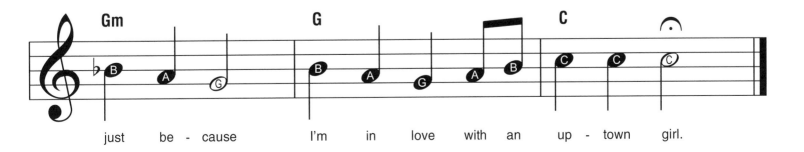

just be-cause   I'm in love with an up-town girl.

Vienna

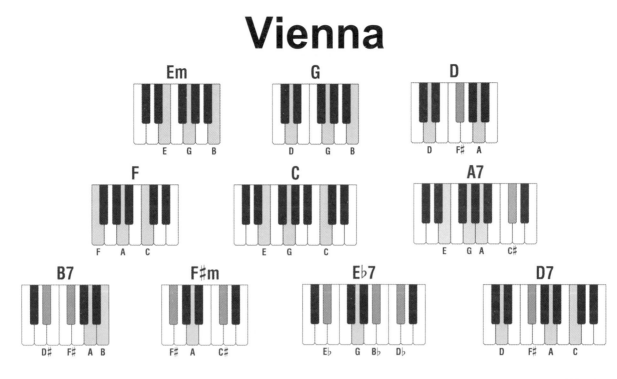

Words and Music by
Billy Joel

Moderate Shuffle

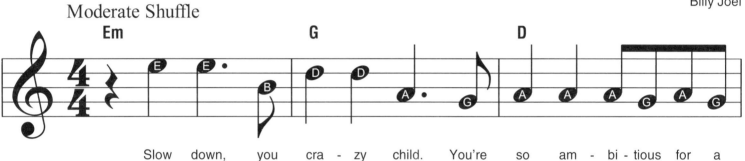

Slow down, you cra-zy child. You're so am-bi-tious for a

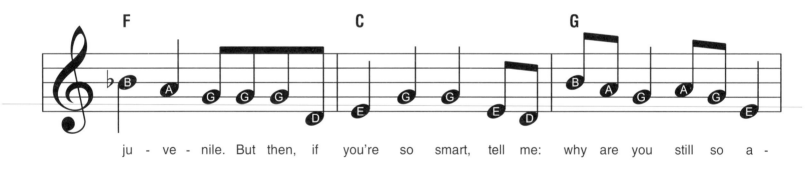

ju-ve-nile. But then, if you're so smart, tell me: why are you still so a-

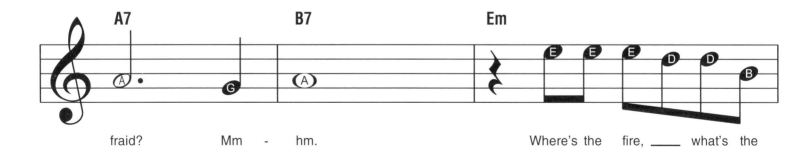

fraid? Mm-hm.   Where's the fire, ___ what's the

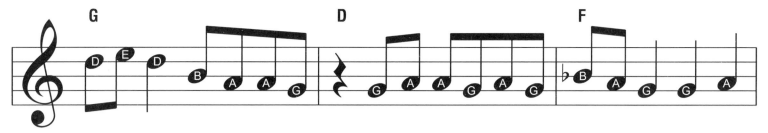

hur - ry a - bout? You bet - ter cool it off be - fore you burn it out. You got

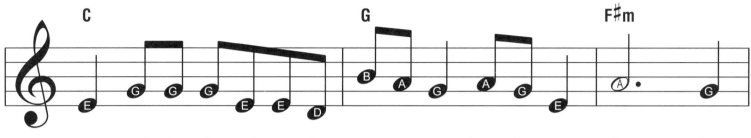

so much to do and on - ly so man - y hours in a day, hey. ___

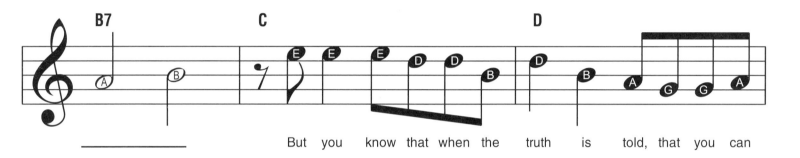

_____ But you know that when the truth is told, that you can

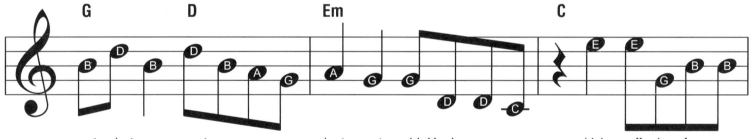

get what you want or you can just get old. You're gon - na kick off be - fore you

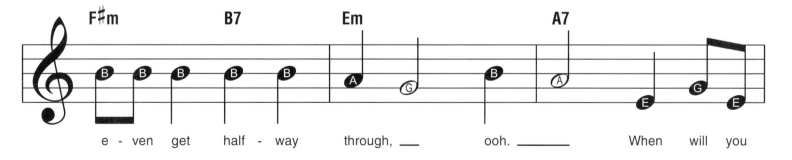

e - ven get half - way through, ___ ooh. _____ When will you

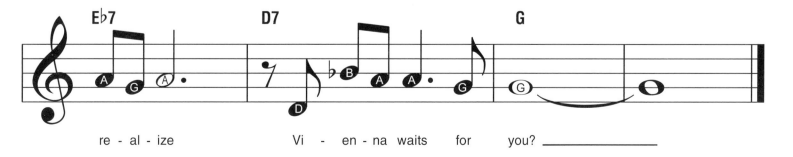

re - al - ize Vi - en - na waits for you? _____

We Didn't Start the Fire

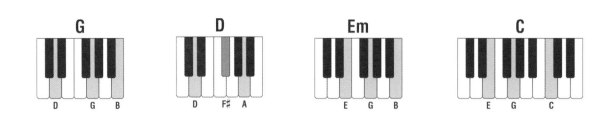

Words and Music by
Billy Joel

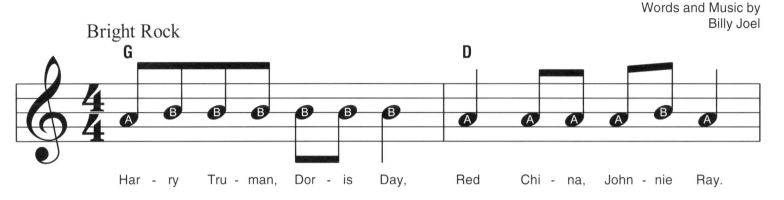

Bright Rock

Har - ry Tru - man, Dor - is Day, Red Chi - na, John - nie Ray.

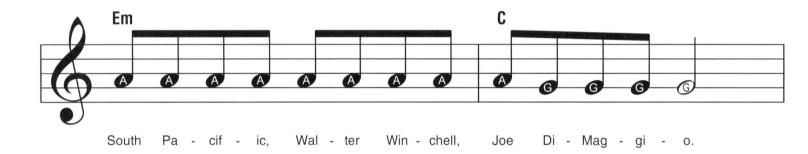

South Pa - cif - ic, Wal - ter Win - chell, Joe Di - Mag - gi - o.

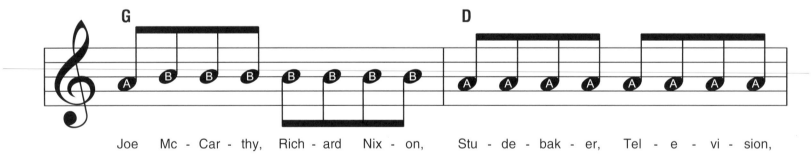

Joe Mc - Car - thy, Rich - ard Nix - on, Stu - de - bak - er, Tel - e - vi - sion,

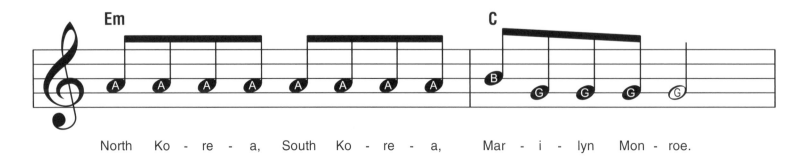

North Ko - re - a, South Ko - re - a, Mar - i - lyn Mon - roe.

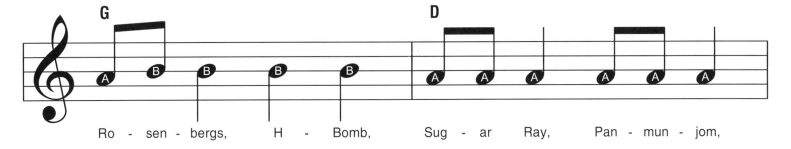

Ro - sen - bergs, H - Bomb, Sug - ar Ray, Pan - mun - jom,

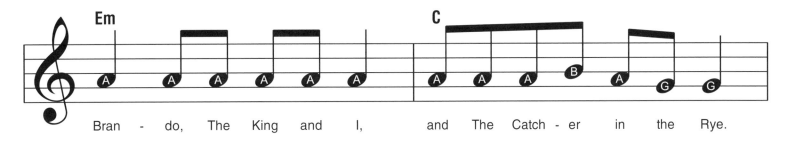

Bran - do, The King and I, and The Catch - er in the Rye.

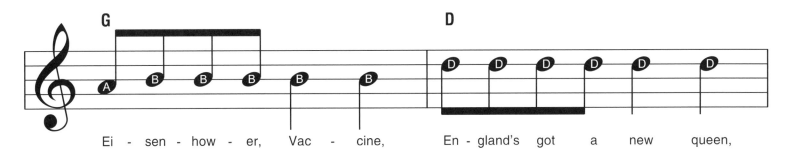

Ei - sen - how - er, Vac - cine, En - gland's got a new queen,

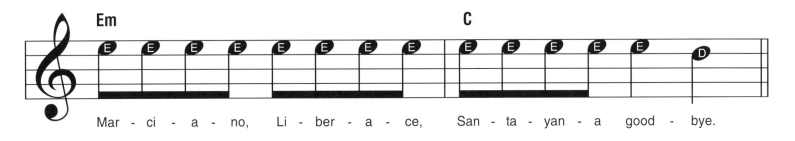

Mar - ci - a - no, Li - ber - a - ce, San - ta - yan - a good - bye.

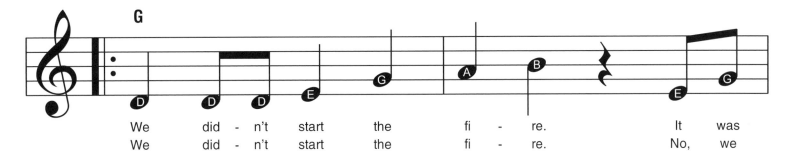

We did - n't start the fi - re. It was
We did - n't start the fi - re. No, we

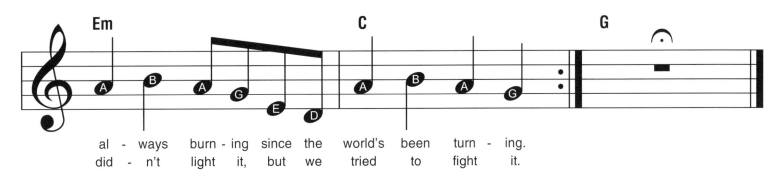

al - ways burn - ing since the world's been turn - ing.
did - n't light it, but we tried to fight it.

You May Be Right

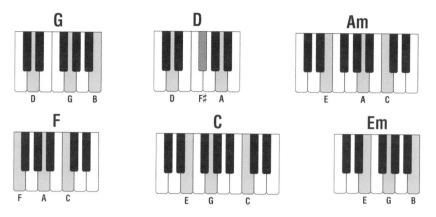

Words and Music by
Billy Joel

Bright Rock

Fri - day night I crashed your par - ty, Sat - ur - day I
strand - ed in the com - bat zone. I walked through Bed - ford

said, "I'm sor - ry." Sun - day came and trashed me out a -
Stuy a - lone, e - ven rode my mo - tor - cy - cle in the

gain. _____ I was on - ly hav - ing
rain. _____ And you told me not to

fun, _____ was - n't hurt - ing an - y - one. _____ And we
drive, _____ but I made it home a - live. _____ So you

SUPER EASY SONGBOOK

It's super easy! This series features accessible arrangements for piano, with simple right-hand melody, letter names inside each note, and basic left-hand chord diagrams. Perfect for players of all ages!

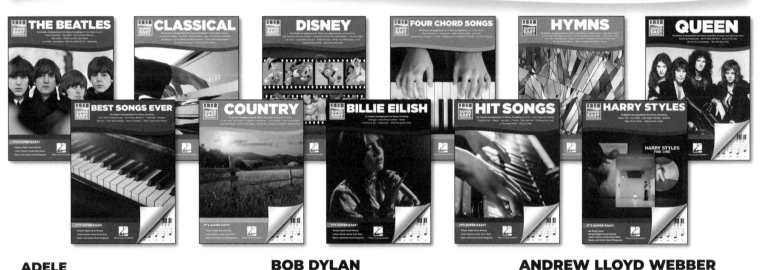

ADELE
00394705 22 songs.....................$14.99

THE BEATLES
00198161 60 songs.....................$15.99

BEAUTIFUL BALLADS
00385162 50 songs.....................$14.99

BEETHOVEN
00345533 21 selections..............$9.99

BEST SONGS EVER
00329877 60 songs.....................$16.99

BROADWAY
00193871 60 songs.....................$15.99

JOHNNY CASH
00287524 20 songs.....................$9.99

CHART HITS
00380277 24 songs.....................$12.99

CHRISTMAS CAROLS
00277955 60 songs.....................$15.99

CHRISTMAS SONGS
00236850 60 songs.....................$15.99

CHRISTMAS SONGS WITH 3 CHORDS
00367423 30 songs.....................$10.99

CLASSIC ROCK
00287526 60 songs.....................$15.99

CLASSICAL
00194693 60 selections...............$15.99

COUNTRY
00285257 60 songs.....................$15.99

DISNEY
00199558 60 songs.....................$15.99

BOB DYLAN
00364487 22 songs.....................$12.99

BILLIE EILISH
00346515 22 songs.....................$10.99

FOLKSONGS
00381031 60 songs.....................$15.99

FOUR CHORD SONGS
00249533 60 songs.....................$15.99

FROZEN COLLECTION
00334069 14 songs.....................$12.99

GEORGE GERSHWIN
00345536 22 songs.....................$9.99

GOSPEL
00285256 60 songs.....................$15.99

HIT SONGS
00194367 60 songs.....................$16.99

HYMNS
00194659 60 songs.....................$15.99

JAZZ STANDARDS
00233687 60 songs.....................$15.99

BILLY JOEL
00329996 22 songs.....................$11.99

ELTON JOHN
00298762 22 songs.....................$10.99

KIDS' SONGS
00198009 60 songs.....................$16.99

LEAN ON ME
00350593 22 songs.....................$10.99

THE LION KING
00303511 9 songs.......................$9.99

ANDREW LLOYD WEBBER
00249580 48 songs.....................$19.99

MOVIE SONGS
00233670 60 songs.....................$15.99

PEACEFUL MELODIES
00367880 60 songs.....................$16.99

POP SONGS FOR KIDS
00346809 60 songs.....................$16.99

POP STANDARDS
00233770 60 songs.....................$16.99

QUEEN
00294889 20 songs.....................$10.99

ED SHEERAN
00287525 20 songs.....................$9.99

SIMPLE SONGS
00329906 60 songs.....................$15.99

STAR WARS (EPISODES I-IX)
00345560 17 songs.....................$12.99

HARRY STYLES
01069721 15 songs.....................$12.99

TAYLOR SWIFT
1192568 30 songs.......................$14.99

THREE CHORD SONGS
00249664 60 songs.....................$16.99

TOP HITS
00300405 22 songs.....................$10.99

WORSHIP
00294871 60 songs.....................$16.99

HAL·LEONARD®

www.halleonard.com

Disney characters and artwork TM & © 2021 Disney

Prices, contents and availability subject to change without notice.